DOING LIFE

DOING LIFE

Dr. Derrick Johnson

Library of Congress Control Number:		2022919179
ISBN:	Hardcover	978-1-6698-4990-2
	Softcover	978-1-6698-4989-6
	eBook	978-1-6698-4988-9

Print information available on the last page.

Rev. date: 11/03/2022

To order additional copies of this book, contact:
Xlibris
844-714-8691
www.Xlibris.com
Orders@Xlibris.com
847279

FOREWORD
(BOOK DEDICATION)

To God Be the Glory

My late mentors:
Rev. Dr. Harrison Fields Sr.
Rev. George B. Harris
Rev. L. V. Scott
Rev. Clennon W. Turner

To my wife, Connie F. Johnson, and my daughters, Constance, Demetria, and Dominique, thank you.

To my mother, Tavia M. Nolen-Johnson; my father, Dwight Johnson (deceased); my sibling and twin, Darryl D. Johnson; and my sister, Via Gladney, thank you for your unending love and support.

To my one and only grandchild, Caleb Derrick Manderville, and to all my biological family across the country, thank you for the love and support throughout these fifty-seven years of my life.

To my line brother, Jon R. Smith, and all my Omega Psi Phi Fraternity Inc. brothers, thank you for always pushing me towards high aspirations.

To my brothers in arm, whom I served proudly within the 82nd Airborne Division, Retired CSMs Kenneth V. Taylor and Anthony R. Johnson, my battle buddy for life, Retired SFC Frank P. Thomas, AATW (Airborne All the Way), Retired SGM Donald Whitmore, and SSG Lynn Henderson, my best man and first battle buddy for life.

To my in-laws, my dear deceased mother-in-law, Ms. Virginia (Bread) Gilmore, sister-in-law Katie Shields, my sister-in-law Jeanette Mullins, my brothers-in-law David and Charlie C. Triplett (both deceased), brother-in-law Robert L. Triplett, and my father-in-law R.J. Triplett (deceased), who is standing by my side as I pen this humble narrative, thank you.

To my host of nieces and nephews, I love you all very dearly.

To my New Birth Missionary Baptist Church family, thank you for the prayers and support that you've shown to me and family. God's Blessings to you all.

Finally, this dedication goes to my grandmother, Ms. Octavics Nolen (Madear) (deceased). I miss you so very much, along with my grandfather, Mr. L. G. Nolen (deceased). I know you both are in the eternal care of God. Forever in our hearts and minds. See you in glory.

GOAL OF BOOK

In this book, the goal is to share my life's journey and to inform you that life is way too brief to ponder on things you have no control over. God wants us to do life with him and not allow life to do us. This is my story about doing life!

INTRODUCTION

"The meaning of life pertains to the significance of living or existence in general. The meaning of life as we perceive it is derived from philosophical and religious contemplation of and scientific inquiries about existence, social ties, consciousness, and happiness." Joseph Campbell says, "The meaning of life is whatever you ascribe it to be. Being alive is the meaning." The Dalai Lama puts it this way: "Our prime purpose in this life is to help others. And if you can't help them at least don't hurt them." Truly, a definition with many different aspects and perceptions of what life consists.

The questions pertaining to life are What in the world does God desire out of my life? What is his designed purpose so blueprinted for my life? Oftentimes we are so hasty to tell God our purpose. Someone once said, "If we want to make God laugh, tell him your plans. I'm of firm belief that God wants us just to do life as he irons out the details of the journey.

Psalm 37:23: The steps of a good man are so ordered by him. Every life, when so directed by God, is so very promising. Regardless how humbling one's beginning may have been, it doesn't erase God's providence for their lives. Jesus's birth in and among barnyard animals was only a genesis to him going to Calvary's ugly cross and, from there, gained his seat on the right hand of the father.

CHAPTER I

A Life Sentence

When we think about a life sentence, most of the world's mindset immediately go to the parameters of the world's penal systems. Systems created to house and contain those individuals who have committed horrendous crimes, such as murder, rape, peddling illegal drugs, crimes against nature, etc. *Merriam-Webster* defines *life sentence* as the "punishment of being sent to prison for the rest of one's life." What a heart-wrenching definition to those of us who, once without Christ as savior, did a life sentence of sorts, trapped in walls and bars of separation, and controlled by a system that literally tears down one's desire to live the life destined by God—a life of joy, comfort, love, care, restoration, and redemption.

A life sentence to those outside the redeeming power of God is truly a life sentence. A life sentence apart from God is a life that is dictated by systems that have been destined to break one's will and desire to live a life orchestrated by God's will. A life sentence with God is a life not free from moments of troubles, but it is a life that allows God to be the wonderful warden of all ups and downs we may experience. A life sentence with God doesn't free us from a trouble-free life, but it does free us from the penalty of sin. Just as a life sentence in the world's penal system was designed as a punishment, so does God's Word, saying he will punish us when we are disobedient to his precepts so outlined in his Word. It's described as chastisement, which is a sign of fatherly correction designed to prevent sin (2 Corinthians 12:7–9), to bless us (Psalm 94:12–13), and to cause submission (2 Corinthians 12:7–10). It is also a sign of sonship (Proverbs 3:11–12), and most importantly, it is God's love (Deuteronomy 8:5).

The world's portrayal of a life sentence is one of harsh, horrible, unlivable conditions. One of relentless violence, sexual immorality, and unforgiving hearts. A life sentence with God, according to John 10:10, is a life that Jesus describes as a more abundant life. What a life sentence! Isn't it comforting to know our earthly life sentence doesn't have to have us be incarcerated by the sin we have committed, doesn't have us on lockdown twenty-four hours a day, and doesn't have us live according to the sounds of cells locking upon our entry into them and sounds of whistles and horns governing our every movement?

In the Garden of Eden, God gave Adam and Eve free reign of everything, except the tree in the midst of the garden; but their lack of obedience limited them and caused them to miss the joys and freedom of life. That disobedience affected mankind from that day until eternity. But thank God for his mercy and compassion. Jesus came on the scene. For God so loved the world (it's the system), he gave us his only begotten son that whoever believes in him should not perish but have everlasting life (John 3:16). But God demonstrates his own love toward us (all mankind) in that while we were still sinners (living a life sentence by worldly standards). Christ died for us.

No longer shall we live a life sentence by worldly standards. Standards created to hold us captive by the choices, calamities, and confusion of this present age. An age of chaos, confusion, and corruption. An age of discrimination, disobedience, and delusional thoughts. An age of racial profiling, rage, and reckless abandonment. An age of a divided nation. Isiah 61:10 says, God proclaims liberty to the captives and the opening of the prison to those who are bound. God expunged the record of those who believe in his son, Jesus Christ, at Calvary. Calvary sealed our records, and now our life sentence is a life free from the bondage of sin's ugly stain.

Chapter II

Life's Genesis

Introduction: My Genesis into This World. May 15, 1965, 6:36 p.m. Life's Inception (Quick, Fast, and in a Hurry)

In the poem penned by the noted poet Paul Laurence Dunbar titled "Life," he speaks of life's joys, tears, laughter, and the realities of our journey in this world. He speaks of the troubles that come along the way as we pilgrim through what the old church used to echo this barren land. No person is exempt from trouble.

Job 14:1 reminds us that a man born of a woman is short of days and full of trouble (HCSB). Job emphatically informs us, life passes us by just as quickly as metro transit travelling at speeds beyond our imaginations. The analogy is, this life goes fast and swiftly. Quick, fast, and in a hurry. We have to climb and ride it, holding on to the powerful aboard unchanging hand of God. That's why we must understand and know who's our conductor of life.

No matter what this life throws, and no matter how fast and swift it may be, God's providence is at work.

Dr. Tony Evans, in his book *Detours*, said this about providence. He said providence is the hand of God in the glove of history. Our lives will be the history of how we trusted to love each other and did his will for our lives. So many people, from the past and the present, live life based on happenstance, which implies that life consequences are to be seen as luck, fluke, fortune, accident, or by chance.

The gospel clearly reminds us in Ecclesiastes 3:1–8 that there are appointed times for everything. God and only God knows the journey of our lives. God can take our bad choices, mistakes, and events unplanned in life and mold them all together to fulfill his purpose and our destiny for his purpose and will. I'm of firm confidence that God is the orchestrator of life. There are no mere coincidences. What may appear to some as random acts or chance is, without a doubt, overseen and overwatched by a God, who is sovereign. God's sovereignty lets us know he is the absolute ruler, conductor, and keeper of life. God's the final say to all that transpires in our lives.

People throughout our society have, both now and in antiquity, seemed to believe that what happens in life takes God by surprise. Just because we're taken by surprise doesn't mean God is. What a phenomenal God he is. God, rest assured, will prevail, and that he is in control, even when life seems out of control.

Life is all about balance. That is why our lives should be lived to the best of our ability to please God. In Ephesians 5:15, Paul's letter to the church at Ephesus says he implores the Christian believers there to be careful how they walk, not as unwise men, but as wise. Paul IOW tells them that in life, one should be wise and careful in all things. Writing from a prison cell, Paul understands that life has no promise, that troubles would befall us; but even when trouble arise, God's providence and sovereignty are and will always be the determining factors of life. Enjoy life, it's too brief not to!

"You make known to me the path of life in your presence is the fullness of joy at your right hand are pleasures forevermore" (Psalm 16:11 ESV). Stay on the path destined by God.

"God will never allow you to go through something you can't handle, and He will not send you into battle without carrying you" (Winnie Mathenge).

Stay upbeat and motivated to run after the life that God has placed before you.

Quick, fast, and in a hurry—that's how life sometimes seems to be! Don't waste your life. Don't be discouraged. You will be rewarded! (Revelation 22:12)

Live your best life. The best life to live is a life that seeks to know God's will and God's way!

CHAPTER III

Let Life Soak In

I sat at my computer some sixteen to eighteen months later. I have to go back in time where we, as a people unknowing for the most part, became engulfed in one of the most baffling pandemics. In this country's history, according to news outlets, what started in late November 2019 broke out in Wuhan, China. CDC officials became aware of the coronavirus on December 31, 2019.

Oftentimes in life, we have to just sit back, and let it all soak in from the mental aspect.

We have to observe and or enjoy something. What a way to look at our circumstances in life. IOW. *Let go.* At the time of the penning of this book, according to Worldmeter, there had been 175,557,138 cases and 3,787,032 deaths worldwide; but on the bright side of those staggering numbers, 159,092,161 have recovered. Let this soak in. A virus that is really untraceable with an unknown genesis and is unforgiven means it can cripple all, regardless of race, creed, religion, or culture.

To this date, as I'm compiling this data for the purposes of this chapter, the USA has had 34,271,741 cases, 613,831 deaths, and 28,274,518 recoveries, which I am included. As I was preparing myself to celebrate Resurrection Sunday, I began to feel weak, fatigued, and just drained. I thought maybe it was because I hadn't long returned from a wedding ceremony in Florida, where the weather was hot, muggy, and humid, only to the return a few days later to LA, where the temperatures were in the lower sixties and midfifties. Unaware of possible exposure, I thought nothing of it. I just assumed I had what we call the common cold. So after letting my uncertainty soak in, my wife and I found ourselves at the nearby ER to be examined, checked, and tested for COVID.

We both were somewhat uneasy. Surely not us. We did all the CDC requirements: wearing a mask, sanitizing our hands often, social distancing, etc. I had taken my first vaccine three days prior (*I'm good*, I kept saying in my mind). "Surely, we should be COVID-free," I personally said to myself. I know my God would not permit me to test positive for COVID that day. Not on Resurrection Sunday, not on the day of his son's, Jesus Christ, death, bruise and resurrection.

As I was letting it all soak, God told me in 2 Timothy 1:7, "For God has not given us a spirit of fearfulness, but one of power, love, and sound judgement" (HSCB). *Spirit* here probably refers to the Holy Spirit. The Greek word translated fearfulness is used in extra-biblical texts to refer to a person who fled from battle. Fearfulness is a strong term for cowardice. If I was not to fall into this category, I had to wait with confidence, regardless of the results. I could have easily said no to the testing and departed to worshipping services. What was supposedly to be a rapid test seemingly took days.

My mind began racing with all kinds of emotions. What if I'm positive for COVID? What if I passed it on to my family, friends, coworkers, church members, etc.? *What if, what if* echoed loudly in my mind. I had to let it all soak in. I said, trust God, Romans 8:28.

Philippians 4:6–7

Soaking it in not only involves observation of things, but it also involves the power of positive thought. Charles R. Swindoll said, "Life is 10 percent what happens to you and 90 percent how you react to it." Things arise in life. Life is not and was not designed to be easy. There will be mishaps, heartbreaks, heartaches, and social injustices and tragedies. Our thoughts can be the difference in controlling what does and does not happen to you. Once one can realize this, we can handle what life throws at us. I had to say, my inner self acting out of fear makes me seem weak. I said, "Self, have faith and hope you can handle whatever challenges that are thrown your way. Soaking it in all means we have let go. It's a process."

The test results process lingered for several hours. Finally, the results were back. My wife and I tested positive for COVID. Needless to say, we both were devastated, not one of us, but both of us. We both kind of slumped down in our chairs and just soaked it all in and said, "Now what?" That is when we went to God and asked him to make sense out of it all.

Treatment and recovery had begun its long tedious journey. After the required quarantine, life appeared to be somewhat back to normal or the new normal, which included vitamins, rest, masks, and social distancing. After following the guidelines set forth by the CDC, it appeared that I was home free. But to my surprise, I once again started to feel sick in my body—cough, fever, night sweats, etc. I said to myself, "Not again." So to the local ER, here I go yet again.

Barely able to support myself, I arrived, and soon thereafter, I was diagnosed with pneumonia. I was immediately sent to the ICU at the request of the doctors there. I'm thinking and letting it all soak in. I begin to once again question God: "Why me, God, why am I here in this place yet again? Have I made you angry? Have I not tried to live by your precepts?"

Once again, I had to inquire in his Word, where it said in 2 Corinthians 4:17, "For our light and momentary troubles are achieving for us an eternal glory that far outweighs them all." Paul, in this verse, speaks about physical, outward suffering. Paul calls it light afflictions, not heavy. Even the worst of our experiences, as compared to eternity, is but for a little while. Our affliction is a cake walk to what others deal. Our affliction is easy compared to what we deserve. Let that soak in. Observe positive thoughts! Enjoy! Let go!

Needless to say, as I recovered from a second round of COVID, I found myself battling heart issues, kidney issues, blood glucose issues, and faith issues. As I spent my days in recovery, I had to rest as much as I could. I had to make countless visits to heart and kidney specialists (they were far from where I lived). I am so grateful that my Wife was my leaning post. She made sure appointments were made on time and meds were taken on time. She did all these tasks despite dealing with and recovering from her bout with COVID. I thank God for my wife, Connie. After thirty-two years of holy matrimony, she still knows what I need. We must always give God the glory for those whom he has given us and appreciate them and tell them thank you!

Thank you, Connie, for being there in one of the most challenging hours of my life. The Bible says in Proverbs 18:22, "Whosoever finds a wife finds a good thing and obtains favor from God" (KJV). Having a caring, compassionate, supportive, and strong support system makes for a steadfast mindset. Having a support system makes this journey called life worthwhile. Special thanks to my niece Tan for travelling from Florida to side in my recovery. Thank God for my daughter's Demetria, Dominique and grandson Caleb for taking care of Paw Paw.

I wanted to ensure that this particular excerpt from an unknown author was a part of this book. I found it as I was looking through some of my old brainstorming thoughts in times past, and I believe that will enrich someone's life as it has on mine.

Life is about different stages, and in each stage of life, no matter its challenges may bring, we have to just slow down and think things through. Thinking things through prevents

Thinking Things Through

Unknown Author

Each stage of life brings with it challenges. The major and minor milestones to remember is:

a. What you face today has already been conquered by millions.
b. Someone's opinion of you is only a fact if you think so.
c. Friends will come and go, but family is present for a lifetime.
d. What you put into your life is what you will get out of it.
e. Every problem has a solution.
f. Every successful solution has been tried time and time again and conquered the problem each time.
g. Your disappointments are not failures but opportunities to conquer defeat.
h. Wrong is wrong, even if everybody does it.
i. Right is right, even if nobody does it.
j. Respect is a gift earned through life trials. No one gives it and no one takes it away.
k. Grow today so you can enjoy success tomorrow.
l. Challenge yourself to see the other side of your temptation
m. Never value fake reflections, fake friends, and fake gold.
n. Value your creator, knowledge, experience, and wisdom. These things you can take everywhere and they will never leave you alone.
o. Life is only one opportunity.
p. You will be dead longer than you will be alive. Are you sure what happens after you die? Spirituality is a choice.

CHAPTER IV

Show Me/Give Me Something in Life

In the previous chapter entry, we talked about letting the circumstances of life as it presents itself to our journey. Let it soak in. But what should our reactions and responses be when things transpire in our lives that are simply so hard to grasp into our rational thoughts? Things like people attempting to sabotage all that we do in deed and not in words only. The hospitality, compassion, care, comfort, and consolation we show to others when we, in fact, need those same sentiments. How hard is it for society to follow the rules for kingdom living? How hard is it for society to treat each other with the attributes of God?

Jesus, in Luke's gospel version of the Sermon on the Plain Mount (Luke 6:20–38), similar to Matthew's account, outlines some simplistic guidance for us as a society to live by, even when we are opposed by those for whatever reason. I've learned some valuable lessons in my short journey thus far in my life. Of all the lessons I've learned, I think the most valuable is that I can't be held responsible for how persons treat me but by how I treat others. That's the golden rule. Love thy neighbor as thyself. The sad flipside to that is this: Many persons have yet to learn how to love themselves. So many people in society are dealing with past betrayal, belittlement, brokenness, back-biting, self-esteem issues, and the list could go on. So many barriers have been constructed in our lives. Dr. Tony Evans, in his book *Your Comeback*, says, "Your past doesn't have to determine your future." That we have become a lone ranger of sorts; that we have separated ourselves from a life that God wants us to enjoy.

I've often found myself at times in a mode of isolation. Isolating myself from family, friends, foes, God, greatness, aspirations, accolades, dreams, desires, love, goals, and even feelings of not deserving God's grace. It is at those times in my life I have to dive into God's love book (Bible) and realize that, even in times of isolation, God's presence is yet there with me. God always shows me and gives me something that reassures me of his everlasting love and care. Oftentimes, during these moments of isolation in my life, I recall King David's moments of isolation, moments of feeling like a burden.

"Cast thy burden upon the Lord and he shall sustain you. He shall never permit the righteous to be moved" (Psalm 55:22). When we give it all to God, he will show you something—he will show you his love and care. He will give you something—his protection and peace. Friends, God is readily available to give you what you need in those moments of isolation. I know you may be saying, "Well, I'm just a loner, I'm not religious, I'm not a people person, I just stay in my lane." That's okay to feel that way. But why remain isolated from the joys of life, isolated from a God that wants to love and care for us?

During my battle with COVID-19 for the second time, I was isolated in a single-room ICU unit. I've never felt isolated in my entire life. No family or friends were readily available to see me, console me, or care for me. Even God felt far from me. But the words of Jesus rained into my heart and mind. "Low I am with you even to the end of the age" (Matthew 20:28b). Once again, God gave me his protection and peace. Once again, God showed me his love and care.

No matter what vicissitudes of life we may face, God shows and gives us his unchanging and unmatched love and care, along with his peace and protection. It may appear to the human sight that the Lord may have your life in shambles. You may not be able to see the bright side. But I assure you, God has not left you in isolation. But his word holds true: "I will never leave you nor forsake you" (Hebrews 13:5b).

What a comforting reassurance we have in God's Word. Even in our moments of feeling isolated, God's presence remains a steadfast and secure stronghold. Isolation is the prime time to understand God's presence when we feel the walls of appear to be crumbling down all around us. Remember, God is getting ready to show us something and give us something—his care, love, peace, and protection.

In this world, in this life, we will have some uncomfortable moments; we will have some unpeaceful times, but Jesus reminds us of the peace left for us in holy writ found in John's gospel, where he says, "Peace I leave with you; my peace I give to you. Not as the world gives do I give to you. Let not your hearts (the seat of our intellect) be troubled neither let them be afraid" (John 14:27). "These things I have spoken to you that in me, you have peace. We all will have tribulation, but be of good cheer I have overcome the world" (John 16:33). Friends, God controls all things! God has big plans for us while we're doing life!

Chapter V

A Homeward-Bound Life

After someone has been proven unjustly sentenced to a life sentence in the world's penal system (oftentimes because of faulty legal representation, racial profiling, unreliable witness whose statements are sometimes fabricated by corrupt law enforcement, and forced or coerced confession), years and decades can pass as a prisoner can be held captive during life. Years and decades of trying to get their cases relooked. Appeals upon appeals, often denied or often ignored. It is during those disappointing rejections that one's hope becomes one's hopelessness, one's trust in what is supposed to be a fair and just system. A system that targets the disenfranchised, the undereducated, the unintellectual, and the underprivileged. A system designed to profit from the incarceration of others. A multimillion-dollar system that attempts to rehabilitate often ends with a revolving door—a door that slams away true and fair justice. Even with a faulty judicial system, there is always somebody advocating unbeknownst the individual's knowledge. We are to be grateful and glad that we have an advocate who is pleading our cases.

Jesus Christ is our greatest advocate. Ephesians 1:7 says, "In him we have redemption through his blood, the forgiveness of sin, according to the riches of his grace." Those who trust in Christ need not worry, even when condemning evidence is stacked against them. God is always gathering conflicting evidence on our behalf that will help us to be homeward-bound. Evidence that will acquit us from the unjust systems that were designed to keep us from being bound for home. A home that he prepared before the foundation of the world. A home filled with comfort, compassion, care, peace, and joy. A home that Christ stress and strain. A home free from troubles and tribulations. A home, Job 3:17–19 tells us, "There the wicked cease from troubling and there the weary are at rest. There the prisoners rest together. They do not hear the voice of the oppressor the small and great are there and the servant is free from his master." *Homeward bound* means reuniting with those we love. *Homeward bound* means a new lease on life from the world's perspective. *Homeward bound* from an eternal perspective means eternal, everlasting life as we reign with the Savior Jesus Christ. No longer on parole in this cruel world, waiting for extradition to glory land. Homeward bound.

CHAPTER VI

God's Guiding Light

The beloved God never promised us that doing life would be without situations and stresses that wouldn't try our faith. God never promised all our days would be bright, absent the dark times. Just as he spoke in Genesis chapter 1, "Let there be light to earth," clothed in darkness, he, too, can bring illumination into each of our lives. Doing life shouldn't always have to be valley experiences David, in one of the most known bible passages Psalm 23, said he walked through the valley; he didn't take residence there. Oftentimes while doing life, we get accustomed to the valley because we feel hopeless despair.

Doing life is not void of those times. Sometimes life does us unfairly in our minds. But God's Word says God is fair because he rains on just as the unjust. God, in his Word, has countless examples of just persons whom life did them unjustly—persons like Moses, Joseph, Isiah, and even his only begotten son, Jesus. But through all their tribulations, they did life according to the superior sovereignty of God, which throws luck and happenstance out of the window. Remember, friends, God is all knowing and God is almighty. Keep doing life and God promises that it will be all worthwhile.

CHAPTER VII

A Prayer *Life*

The challenges that we all face and that we all must overcome are the things in life that we can improve. Friends, life, in a nutshell, comes down to the choices and decisions that we are to make on a daily basis. Whether you believe it or not, we are who we are based on the decisions we've made. The wonderful news is that God has made it clear in his Word that he wants the best for us all.

Jeremiah 29:11 says he knows the plans for us, which include peace and not evil; he wants to give us a bright future and a hope. This requires that we seek his will for our lives. That's why a prayer life is so very imperative. The Word of God places much emphasis on it.

First Thessalonians 5:17 says we should pray constantly. It is our duty to pray. Prayer promotes fellowship with God. Prayer draws us closer to God and closer to his will for our lives.

James 4:8 says, "Draw near to God and he will draw near to us." God's aim for us is to have fellowship and fellowship with him. The God of this universe wants all the decisions and choices we need to make in this life to begin with seeking his will and way for us, to begin with prayer. We must know and realize that God longs to speak with us daily. Praying is not us trying to move God. Praying is following God's directions that he has spoken to us. He orders us to pray.

Luke 18:1 says men should always pray, not as a get-out-of-jail free card, but as a means for us to seek his will for our lives. There are no rules or restrictions. God is not concerned with fancy intellectual words as he is about the condition of our hearts and honesty.

Prayer allows the burdens of life to be placed on the shoulders of God Almighty. I've learned to pray to God and to praise him in advance for working out things in my life with his unlimited power and precise. When we allow this, we truly know that all things are working for the good and for his purpose in our lives.

CHAPTER VIII

A Prayer

When our choices and decisions in this life begin with prayer, we will be able to say without any doubt that God did it. When prayer is first and foremost the cares of this life, life will not overwhelm us.

"But seek first the kingdom of God and his righteousness and all these things shall be added to you" (Matthew 6:33). Even Jesus drew great strength from his Heavenly Father through prayer. The great news is, we must believe and trust God. Believe, God has made it clear what he wants for us. "Trust in the Lord will all your heart and lean not on your own understanding in all your ways acknowledge him and He shall direct your paths" (Proverbs 3:5–6).

Prayer begins with trusting God. The God who created all things. The God who knows all things. The God who controls all things. The God who can do anything but fail us. The God who wants fellowship and followship from humanity. It all begins with a prayer life. Just a little talk with the master throughout our daily lives makes it all right. Prayer is nothing more than just a request to God, be it in secret, family, or a group. It is not to be done in doubt, pride, or selfishness, but done with a pure heart. We all need a prayer life.

In the words of Andrew Murray, who was a Christian pastor, writer, and South African educator "Prayer is simply asking and receiving from God".

God has plans to prosper us. God has plans to love and care for us despite us. God has plans to always be able for us. God has plans to never leave us or forsake us. More importantly, God has plans to see us through all the choices and decisions we must make while doing life with him!

Be blessed this day and forevermore. Please carve out time daily in your life for prayer. Doing life is a sum total of our choices and decisions we encounter and have to make. I promise you, my friend, your life will never be the same. Anything God has orchestrated for your life will not leave your life. It will all work to line up with God's purpose for your life. Just see it through!

Great is thy faithfulness. If you're reading this book, let me tell you it's going to get better. Keep praying and trusting in our merciful God. The Prophet Jeremiah declared in Lamentations that God's mercies are new every day. Even in our times of lament, God's mercy is renewed daily. Today is your day to begin a prayer life and let God work it all out. What a compassionate God.

Life
Paul Laurence Dunbar

A crust of bread and a corner to sleep in.
A minute to smile and an hour to weep in.
A pint of joy to a peck of trouble.
And never a laugh but the moans come double; and that is life!

A crust and a corner that love makes precious
With a smile to warm and tears to refresh us;

And joy seems sweeter when cares come after,

And a moan is the finest of foils for laughter
And that is life!

CHAPTER IX

Don't Waste Your Life

If I could advise or give advice to everyone that is on God's green earth, it is this: Don't waste your life on senseless and trivial things that don't mean a hill of beans to your destiny. Some people waste countless amounts of time in their lives, lying dormant in life. Some people have no goals, no motivation, no steadfastness or spiritual stamina. Some people would rather live and let live their lives haphazardly without any regards to what God desires from them. Some people leave this world without pursuing their dreams and desires, as it pertains to God's will for their lives.

I do understand that we live in an unjust culture. Everyone is not treated fairly according to the standards outlined by the world we reside in. But that's not a valid excuse for us to waste our lives by settling for the status quo. God has so given us equally the grace to accomplish a life filled with purpose. God is not a respecter of persons. The problem that exists for a lot of persons is this. They have self-esteem issues and feelings of unworthiness. God has created us all for his glory.

Our lives should be lived to glorify God. We're to live life in a way that brings glory to God. We achieved this by communing daily with God through prayer, fellowship, and private devotion/study. God wants us to live fulfilled lives that, when it's over down here, we can hear "well done"! If we want to make sure we don't waste our time, first, we must remain encouraged. We will reap if we faint not. Keep serving. Keep doing good and keep working for the Lord. Secondly, stay focused. Avoid distractions from what the world throws at us. Lastly, don't waste opportunities to sow seeds that will produce a hearty harvest.

Hebrews 13:2 says, "Do not neglect to show hospitality to strangers for by this some have entertained angels without knowing it."

Every time we get a chance to help someone, show love to our neighbor, and share the good news with the hurting, we glorify God. My prayer is that we all live our lives without wasting our lives. Live in obedience to God, and when we do, we can experience a close spiritual thriving and transforming relationship with God.

There are only two ways to use your time: wisely or foolishly. Don't waste your life.

CHAPTER X

Proud Moments in My Life

Over these five decades and two and a half years of my life, I've experienced some highs and lows. The stillbirth death of twin boys my wife was allowed by God to carry for one trimester was one, if not the most, devastating event that has happened in my life. That single event in my life caused me to realize that God is the creator and giver of all life. Even though that event was meant by the enemy to discourage and disappoint my wife and I, we knew that God's plans and divine purpose for us wasn't over. Several years later, he blessed us with two healthy baby daughters. Despite them being born early and 364 days apart, it was the proudest moment of our lives. To hold them and to cherish their genesis into this world made the both of us proud to be seen worthy by God to be parents. Moments like these outweighs the sadness of losing twin boys. Moments like these help us both to be grateful and thankful to the Lord.

I believe we all have proud moments in life. For some, it could be educational goals, financial goals, personal and professional goals, marriage, etc. But for me, the birth of my children will always be the proudest moment of my life. With all that God has allowed me to attain in my life, being a parent is the proudest moment for me, aside from accepting Jesus Christ as my Lord and Savior at the age of ten. Parenthood has been and is still a proud moment in my life. Parenting is a lifetime task. To watch my children grow into young, intelligent, productive, professional, respectful, resourceful, and goal-oriented young women is truly a blessing from God. I just remain hopeful and prayerful to God that I still do my part.

Proverbs 16:22 says, "Train up a child in the way they should go and when they grow old they shall not depart from it."

Constance, Demetria, and Dominique, keep trusting in God to lead and guide each of your footsteps. Don't try to figure it by yourselves. Let God's Word be your guide. Psalm 119:105 assures you all that his Word is a lamp to your feet and a light to your path. To my dearest grandson, Caleb "Derrick" Paw Paw, my prayer is that he will live a life that serves as a priestly example to you, an example of what he (God) wants for your life. I pray for your Godly protection, and prosperity that comes only from God. You, too, are another proud moment in my life. That's my inheritance.

Proverbs 25:12–13 tells us this: Who is the man that fears the Lord? Him shall he teach in the way he chooses. He himself shall dwell in prosperity and his descendants shall inherit the earth.

To all who read this book, keep doing life and watch God give you a life that will be filled with his promises. Promises that will not be broken. Promises of provision, protection, and victorious living. Romans 8:37–39 says, "Yet in all things we are more than conquerors through Him who loved us. For I am persuaded that neither death, nor life, nor angels, nor principalities, nor powers, nor things present nor things to come, nor height nor depth, nor any other created thing, shall be able to separate us from the love of God, which is in Christ Jesus our Lord." What a wonderful promise. God's promises are irrevocable. God's promises are his Word.

About the Author

Dr. Derrick D. Johnson

Dr. Derrick D. Johnson was born in Memphis, Tennessee, to Dwight Johnson and Tavia M. Nolen-Johnson, the second child of twin boys. He matriculated through the Tennessee Public School System. He was a former US Marine and retired army master sergeant. A combat veteran (two times), Dr. Johnson was called to the ministry on June 21, 2001, under the leadership of the late Rev. L. V. Scott.

Dr. Johnson has a steadfast love for God's people. Dr. Johnson is the former pastor of Ellen Burr Missionary Baptist, where he served faithfully for ten years. He currently serves as a pastor at the New Birth Missionary Baptist in Leesville, Los Angeles, serving the local community along with the servicemen and women at Fort Polk Military Installation. Dr. Johnson has a great number of accomplishments, as well as earned degrees to undergird God's anointing in his life.

Made in the USA
Columbia, SC
05 June 2025

58961704R00031